THE MUSTARD SEED

[a natural foods grocer]

a verse memoir

x _Sugar le Fae_

DESIGN BY Theo Hall

Publisher's Cataloguing-in-Publication Data

le Fae, Sugar
   Mustard seed / written by Sugar le Fae / designed by Theo Hall
ISBN: 978-1-953932-18-1

1. Poetry - General 2. Poetry: LGBTQ+ 3. Biography & Autobiography: Personal Memoirs I. Title II. Author

Library of Congress Control Number: 2023931754

In 2016, I was teaching as an adjunct English instructor at Nashville State. Student debt had tanked my credit. I couldn't afford food, much less, an apartment or a car. I was sleeping on a friend's couch. By happy chance, I secured a room at the French House—an unassuming queer commune in west Nashville. To subsidize my teaching habit, I cashiered part-time at a nearby 'natural foods grocer.' For a year, I wrote daily observations on the backs of trashed receipts; this verse memoir is the result. Names have been changed.

Table of Contents

1. The Mustard Seed

Head Cashier	3
Facing	4
Kree	5
The Circle-Jerk Boys	6
Customer Service	7
Johnny from Deli	8
After the Lunch Rush	9
Bagging	10
Liberty Head Nickel	11
The Mange in Manager	12
'Work' Luke	13
My Pink Pussy Hat	14

2. The French House

French House: Sapphics	17
Sisters (1)	18
Green Room	19
A Body in the Dark	20
Skip-a-Boo	21
The Player Piano	22
Sisters (2)	23
The Plague of Ladybugs	24
Self-Talk	25
Eating Rocks	26
Family Dinner	27
Patrice	28

3. More Mustard

Buffalo Nickel   31
Receipts   32
Nametags   33
Store Radio   34
The Cashier as Art Critic   35
Asking for ID   36
Chels   37
Lament   38
Mid-Shift   39
Rose-Marie's Man-Hands   40
How to Take an Hour Break   41
Walking While White   42

4. Loose Ends

Red Door   45
The Attic   46
Faerie Potluck   47
Vanishing Act   48
Luke Leaves for New York   49
False Buddha   50
Professor Plum   51
Mermaids   52
Still-Life   53
Hiring for Manager   54
Counting My Till   55
Masc   56

NOTES   59
ACKNOWLEDGMENTS   61

1.
The Mustard Seed

[a Natural Foods Grocer]

Head Cashier

Since Carl asked the new girl
to act as Head Cashier,
my morale's been in the gutter.
I've worked here 8 months,
longer than any other cashier.
I've never called-out, never

been late. Got a 98 on my eval.
Since the last manager
talked down her nose at me,
I've resigned trying hard.
Some days, I spend the whole
drive to work stifling dread.

Followed by the guilt
about how good I've got it.
I steal organic coconut water
and cheese-sticks all shift.
Since my brother helped elect
a fascist president, I've lost

the power to fake my feelings.
Even my well-meaning
friends police my demeanor.
Ronnie from Supplements
never fails to ask what's wrong
when she sees me cleaning.

FACING

You can face your fears,
face facts, face an audience.
Here at the Mustard Seed,
we face merchandise
—face it forward
so customers can read
names, flavors, varieties.
Soymilk, vegan sushi, wine,
coffee station carafes,
condiments in the café.
Anything unsightly
is cleaned or carted away.
Customers don't want
to know who made lunch,
what it takes to make it
into work each week.
A place where words are
turned, where you have to
face what you can't
have—where facing it
means making it face you.

KREE

Kree tells me about her car
accident six months ago,
how she broke her eye-socket,
needed speech therapy—
her hundred-thousand-dollar
medical bills and legal fees,
and now it turns out

that the jerk wasn't insured.
We're both poor, both
working here, she knows that.
She just wants someone to
commiserate, wants her words
to be heard. I nod, listen.
She cries alone on the patio

for most of her break.
When she returns, rosy-eyed
to her register, I offer her
chocolate. She passes, calls
to the next customer in my line
(the words she'd love to hear):
I can help you over here.

THE CIRCLE-JERK BOYS

They always want receipts.
Men whose mothers dress them
in button-ups and tasteless ties.
Dudes who broker firms

in this yuppie hub of Nashville.
High-rises, high-ballers, Irish yogis.
Lunch is the new circle-jerk.
These particular guys are nice,

good-looking. They come
in once or twice a day in packs
of four or five. The cute brunette,
probably my favorite, is scared

of me. I sense it. He winces
when we lock eyes, avoids my line.
Do I remind him of that friend
he got caught with one time?

Customer Service

Some straight guys aren't gay.
They're just really excited
that I'm gay, and they want me
to know. It's one more way
they avoid empathy. A gay cashier!
with a buzz-cut and nail-polish.
They can't believe their luck.
They laugh and flirt outrageously.
It's one more way to objectify.
Take this guy in my line recently,
adorable, twentysomething,
howling as I tell the girl
in front of him I'm lesbian
on top, cowboy on the bottom.
When it's his turn, he tells me
he just returned from Cali.
When I ask him why, he smiles,
looks down shyly. A girl, he says.
Then, catching my eye,
Guess I should know better.
Can't help you there, I tell him.
He hasn't stopped laughing.
Plato famously claimed
that lust can lead us to God,
but it also keeps us beasts.
When he forgets his credit card,
I find him outside with two dudes.
He yanks it thankless and turns.

Johnny from Deli

In many ways, Johnny from Deli
is a prototypical white dude.
Fun-loving, scruffy, brooding.
He's got this drunk uncle charisma
that gets him by. Plus, he's cute.
He's everyone's secret crush
but won't date any of us.

Behind the Deli or Juice Bar,
he's in sight of register 1.
It's really the only good thing
about running 1. And puzzling
why we lock eyes so often.
But whether or not he may be
a six-pack away from gay,

he's mulling over something
sad and fundamental that pings
something similar in me.
Not to mention that he's hung-
over every shift. I've noticed time
and again how much I'm
attracted to my own sadness.

After the Lunch Rush

The lady with brain cancer
came through my line again today
in her knit cap and sweatpants,

apologizing for her cancer
if her manner seemed erratic,
leaving to milk and sugar

a coffee, while a line
of people waited.
Frustrated but patient,

I offered to carry her
groceries out to her car,
but she was taking the bus.

I wondered if cancer
had clarified or confused her
counting out exact change.

Was it at last an answer
—a visceral resolve to live or
the sadness she'd been waiting for?

BAGGING

I don't need to brag, but I'm a master bagger.
No one has to ask me to bag their meat
separately, or double-bag their walk home.
I bag all bottles sideways to distribute the weight.
While you confer with the card-reader,
I'm stacking strata in my head: a tarot spread.
First, the Two of Water Bottles, prostrate

on the bottom, overturned but unspilt.
Then the Fruits of Labor: apples, oranges,
cherry tomatoes, cotton candy grapes
washed invisible of their Brown toil.
Reversed: the Fruits of Labor are unsellable,
bruised or ugly—juiced or (rarely) fed to the staff.
The Four of Soup-Cups goes

below To-Go boxes floated soft as UFOs.
Reversed: these Paper Lanterns will. spill. lava.
And obviously, Cold attracts Cold.
Glass under Plastic under Paper under Bread.
My trainees can read carts like star-charts.
The same physics built the pyramids.
All those years of Tetris have finally paid off.

LIBERTY-HEAD NICKEL

Checking out a customer, I broke
a roll of nickels and out she fell.
I thought she was a peso
and set her aside till after the rush.
Her reverse was less corroded,
easier to read: a Roman V inside
a Greek wreath, circled by her owner's

name: United States of America.
Only then did I notice her,
searching the shine for her cameo:
her scarred, hard edges of light,
that far-away look still discernible
in her upturned gaze, the suppleness
where nose meets cheekbone.

America, France, Rome—
Liberty was always Apollo in drag,
the lost Colossus of Rhodes;
Helios, god of the sun and prophesy,
crowned in spikes of light,
who straddled the harbor nude
till an earthquake shook him down.

Her proud countenance,
struck within earshot of the Civil War,
is visible only at a certain slant.
'Liberty' shorn from her coronet,
13 stars halo her loose hair.
And beneath her severed head,
the year, last number rusted-over.

THE MANGE IN MANAGER

For most of my tenure
at the Mustard Seed,
Carl was my favorite manager.
Easygoing, a plebe
like the rest of us.
He left us to our duties.
One night, though, early on,
he scheduled me to close
alone without warning.
Closing chores are no joke.

Cleaning the aisles,
the café, and the bathrooms
while cashiering alone?
But Carl promised to help me.
Then, he tells me to drink
a beer of my choice
from a paper cup.
'With a lid,' he repeats.
I'm not much of a drinker,
but a free drink is free.

After that, Carl vanished,
despite calls on the intercom.
Later, while I mopped
the café, he shakes my cup.
Finish this, he scoffs,
leaving me a second beer.
Closing took so long,
I missed my bus. Walking
home drunk was a headache
I haven't forgotten.

'Work' Luke

As often as he comes
around, you'd think
we were fucking.
When he shows
up drunk at my piano,
having defended
my honor to his father,
I wonder if we're
secretly in love.
Since his promotion

to Head Cashier,
we chat less at work.
We get along best
getting stoned
in my bed / room.
Mostly joking,
I think—What if
the one straight guy
I don't try to fuck
ends up being *the one?*

MY PINK PUSSY HAT
—for Jonny Gray, who knitted it

The night I lost my pussy hat,
having missed the last bus,
I had to walk home after closing.
I thumbed one woolen corner
in a pocket and forgot it.
I wore that hat everywhere.
To the Women's March in D.C.

To New Orleans to toast
St. Brigid. Back to Nashville,
where I wore it behind a register
every day late into the summer.
I touted it at Trump rallies.
Protested oil pipelines.
Marched for migrants' rights.

I donned it as a drag-nun,
raising funds for queer youth.
I lived more life in that hat
than I knew I could. Stood up
taller when I wore it, was kinder.
It's hard to imagine losing it.
Maybe some possessions,

like people, enter and leave
our lives with purpose.
I passed the Edgehill projects.
Maybe a girl found it, pink
on the sidewalk. Her mother,
seeing SISTER stitched across,
washed it and let her keep it.

2.
The French House

I say, someday they'll remember us.
−Sappho

French House: Sapphics

Welcome to the inn at the end of the world.
Home for lost girls. Hostel to wayward strangers.
House Rule 1: Above all, be considerate.
House Rule 2: Don't waste.

Jocelyne sifts through trash on the lawn if need be,
freer on hands and knees than I'll ever be.
Rule 2b: Excess dishwater should be
fed to the houseplants.

Rule 3: Clean-up after yourself and your guests.
No one wants ants. Jocelyne discourages food
upstairs but will usually leave you be
if your room is clean.

Rule 4: Finish what you start. Set intention.
Dry your laundry on the porch if it's warm out.
Jocelyne's always rearranging something.
This house is her spouse.

SISTERS (1)

Sister Mish dumpster-dives
Trader Joe's so often,
they've started leaving her
snacks like an alley cat.
She's *hurt* herself diving!
Schlepping the dive's finds
to Jocelyne's kitchen,

she cleans her catch, leaves
chips, hummus, cheese,
sparkling water in the fridge.
One day, Mish pulled up
with seven buckets of irises
leftover after a banquet
—Such bounty of beauty!

By the time I returned
my teacup to the dishrack,
Jocelyne had grown
a garden in the house
of vases and mason jars,
like a painter studying light
inside her still-life.

Green Room

When Jocelyne offered me
the Green Room, pale olive
with a desk, I agreed
before she finished asking.
I'd been sleeping on a couch,
teaching English Comp
two busses away. I knew
this house. I'd partied here
with faeries for years—
never even went upstairs,

deterred by the bright
Residents Only sign.
This place is sacred space.
I wouldn't think to live here.
Before 440 (and the now
forgotten trollies), when west
Nashville was still pastoral,
a wealthy, white doctor
shot quail for his breakfast
from this stone tower.

By the time Jocelyne,
an immigrant hairdresser,
bought it in the 70s for $6K,
it was condemned, a shell
she could fill and did,
birthing her second girl
in this very room, picking
glass from the grass for years.
I don't mind a few
missing windowpanes.

A Body in the Dark

I'm too many men's
maybe if their girlfriend
leaves them.
I look like a man.
By every metric, I am.
I never thought I wasn't,
but I'm not.

Everybody knows,
who talks to or watches me
walk or gesture.
Even in my boy clothes.
So, I'm genderqueer.
Because trans-feminine
with no desire to transition

is a mouthful.
And I want to feel small.
To be spooned,
or to spoon a man
like a woman spoons a man
when he doesn't know
he wants her to.

SKIP-A-BOO

Every other week or so,
Jocelyne and I play Skip-Bo,
three games in a row.
Skip-a-Boo, she says in French.
We don't have to pay much
attention. Jocelyne deals
the deck before I can shuffle.

My grandpa taught me cards
when I was tall enough
to take his temper.
No one else would be his partner.
He learned to card-shark
on his parents' farm
and later in the South Pacific.

Jocelyne's on a streak
after stalling for a few hands.
T'anks 'eaven! she cries.
I slice cold apples, reading her
Norman Rockwell calendar.
She leaves for Paris soon.
I hate taking care of her plants.

It's your turn, she calls.
I sit, draw, and block her.
You make your grandfather proud,
she says, laughing in French.
The first night I moved in,
she won three rounds.
The house keeps balance.

The Player Piano

J's piano is drunk
with age, muddy and lush.
It hasn't played music-
scrolls in a century,

though doorknobs linger
vestigial, that once opened
on hole-punched rolls.
Summers especially,

keys stick or die,
swelling with the weather.
Most pianos plead to be
heard, stirred, shaken

till they wake the neighbors.
Not Jocelyne's. Dead tree
with teeth—it sleeps
with the birdsong.

One bite can return a tune
to fingers after a decade.
Or wipe from a mind
notes it wrote yesterday.

Sisters (2)

When Sister Mish visits
from the Faerie Mountain,
she claims the couch.
When she stays a few days,
she spreads out, lives in
her living room apartment
like a museum piece.

Sister obliges me to play
the piano, hums along
when she knows the song.
Today, she's in town
to get an old, gold filling
pulled at the dental school,
and catch a matinee.

Her myriad eyeglasses
bespeckle the coffee table.
Tonight, she'll fill the fridge
with perfectly good food
from local dumpsters.
In one night, she'll feed
the house for weeks.

THE PLAGUE OF LADYBUGS

came in with the cold-front
and my sinus infection, driven
by an early frost, spilling
from the ceiling-fan,
transiting plaster like planets.
Jocelyne and the others
aren't as bothered.
I lined the windowsills
with lemon-rinds and cloves,
slid the bed from the wall.

Every night, I suck up bugs
with the vacuum hose
like the horn of judgment.
Every morning,
fresh constellations.
They bleed when scared
—that yellow trail they leave
is blood, not pee.
They leach an earthy scent
that sallows the pillows.

Having stripped the house-
plants of aphids, these ladies
stalk across the ceiling,
falling into flight
with a click, the filmstrip
slip of their wings, then silence.
No recompense. No lesson.
We're here for the same
reason: to live a little
longer than our season.

SELF-TALK

Why do you keep getting high
if it makes you shake like you're dying?
Makes your hurt churn, your hands

numb, your legs jump like Thumper?
—Haven't you been writing
all these years to calm the fuck down?

Already regretting the inevitable living?
Your whole life avoiding what
you couldn't ask—Who touched you

as a child? Why do you love men
who love women? Haven't you failed
even to finish this poem?

EATING ROCKS

You had to be taught
not to eat rocks.
Left alone, you'd hurt
yourself or worse.

Now that you know
better, you break rules
just to break
something. You take

your mother's pills.
You drink coffee
all night writing poetry.
You jog in the dark

in your crop-tops.
As if you never stopped
eating rocks—as if
you had to weigh

yourself down to stay.

Family Dinner

We meet up after work
Thursday evenings
to cook whatever food
the new kid isn't allergic to,
to dish and nosh—
Ronnie's Thai fried-rice.
My attempt at vegan
shepherd's pie. Spaghetti
squash with sauce.
But mostly, we potluck.

None of us make enough
to shop at our store,
even with our employee
discount. We eat free
samples for lunch.
We scour for expired dates.
Once a week, we feast
on mark-outs and cheap wine,
clandestine as a kitchen
of witches. Fae for a night.

Luke was here so often,
Jocelyne offered him a room.
Now, we stay up late,
talking, drawing, stoned
on Bowie and poetry.
He's not much of a cook,
but he's good for whatever
last-minute ingredient.
The new kid is always late
and always grateful.

PATRICE

Jocelyne's daughter sold me
a 1997 green Geo Metro
for $700: broken radio,
one rear-door that won't open,
but it passed the Emissions Test
and starts reliably.
Mom helped me buy it.
I named him Patrick in French.
My world-weary drag queen:
old, slow, and painted to be seen.
Ronnie told me later
that all the Patrices she knows
are Black ladies at church.
Even better, I said.

Mustard Seed employees
shell-out $20/month
to park in a lot down the street.
I parked Patrice at the store
as long as I could, green sheen.
But Corporate noticed
and threatened to tow me.
I had to drive home and bus back.
3 weeks it took for my pass.
Like me, Patrice survived Spring,
wheezing at stoplights,
easy to spot in a lot.
2 miles and back for 6 months.
Never locked. Uninsured.

3.
More Mustard

BUFFALO NICKEL

Half-dissolved, he spills
from a roll of nickels,
spitting into my till:
a white man's caricature,
Native of no tribe, generic
chieftain stereotype,
feathers, leather, braids,
82-years-old, decades
of sweat and slot machines,
a lozenge on the tongue
of good, Christian charity,
too thin to stand up.
I buy him for five cents
from the change cup.

On the back, a buffalo
mourns his horns and tail,
worn away clink by clink
on trolleys, sidewalks,
dulled like sea glass
passed between hands.
His worth certainly hasn't
worn off the auction block.
Nor his owner's slogan:
'One of many' stacked on
his back like a joke.
Flip to know your fate:
life inside a sniper scope,
your head on a plate.

RECEIPTS

We were slammed. I was scanning
this couple's groceries, focused,
head-down, chatting with the wife,
when I noticed the husband:
head shaved, eyes sharp.
How long had he been watching me?
I must've jerked backwards
because he leaned in. Amanda,
he said, meet Zach, we used to be
classmates. Oh, she said. Nice
to meet you. Yes, I said, smiling,
checking her birthdate for the wine.
How are you, Zach? he asked,
half-yelling at me like a dad.

I turned to his wife, face-first
in her purse, and read out the total.
Years passed as she fought
the card-reader. I can still see him
drinking 'real' tequila sunrises
till dawn on my floor, making out
in the bathroom on New Year's Eve,
wandering into the woods
through strangers' backyards
on Spring Break, tripping shrooms.
Spooning nude in his dorm
was as far as we would go.
No wife will ever know him like I do.
I handed her the bags, and let go.

Nametags

According to lore, my dad,
23, an American MP stationed
at Soesterberg Air Base
near Amsterdam,
baby-faced in 1983,
working the nightshift,
flipping through an old dictionary,
found Zachariah
and called my mom,
another American MP,

asleep and very pregnant,
to say he'd found my name.
Mom, 19, hair in two loose braids,
was too Catholic to know
romance from radio.
Dad called back
five minutes later to tell her
he liked Zachary better,
because it's easier to spell
—and doesn't sound so gay.

Whether she laughed
or hung-up, I don't know.
Turns out, Zachary
means Sugar in Greek.
Think: sucre, azúcar, saccharin.
Sugar was queer
as a summer snowstorm
all around them, coffee to coffee,
if only they'd listen.
In Dutch, it sounds like sucker.

STORE RADIO

If we lived in a queer world,
it wouldn't have taken me
33 years to recognize
the inescapable queerness
of Elvis singing 'Hound Dog.'
I hear that damn song
every other hour at work.

I've known my share
of lowdown, oversexed
men like the one Big Mama
Thornton growled at
snooping round her door,
four years before Elvis.
But it didn't dawn on me

till today (hearing his cover
for the third time) that
if we lived in a queer world,
'Hound Dog' would've
been a queer anthem.
Of course, in a queer world,
Big Mama would've been

on Ed Sullivan, hip-
shaking the censors crazy
to cheers of queer kids.
Of course, in a queer world,
there'd be no straight men
or censorship. Nothing
to hide us from who we are.

THE CASHIER AS ART CRITIC

I know it's summer because Marco, the
'Art and Marketing Department,' is
sticking a hundred red and green post-
its in the shape of tomatoes on the
frontend windows. Sometimes, he takes
pics of kale chips or gluten-free
macaroons for the website. He gets
paid salary to do this. He used to suck
Kip's dick, the owner. Whether he still
does, I don't know. But we've all seen
their speedo shots from years ago. At
$10.50/hour, I make more cashiering
than teaching college English. I know
it's been slow because I'm gawking at
Marco on his step-ladder, wasting all
that paper. His tomatoes will never
grow / old, but he'll throw them away
before the next football game or fed-
eral holiday. Pixilated, they glow in the
afternoon sun. Outside, it's a nice day.

ASKING FOR ID

Some customers laugh.
Some puff up their chests
like chimps and stomp
out, howling. But they all
come back eventually,
IDs in hand. Tennessee
hired a minor to buy beer,
and now we always ID.
There's nothing I can do.
Even if you're elderly,
or clearly a war vet.
I still have to card you,
especially if my boss
is standing behind me.

CHELS

Now that the boys are in preschool,
my sister drives up twice a week
to smoke weed and walk
the late-Victorian neighborhoods
behind Belmont University.
We critique design, aesthetics,
landscaping. Four miles
down around campus,
past the Thai Market, and back.
At 5'2, Chels has rushed
her whole life just to keep up
with dad, me, her husband, twins.
Returning, we round the bend
sober, sweaty, and hungry.
She drives me to work early,
and we eat free before my shift.
Circling the salad bar,
we pack our plates with greens,
olives, hummus, the day's protein,
oh and that soy/ginger dressing!
Chels prefers an Hi-Ball energy drink
to my reishi mushroom, super-herb,
chocolate coconut-milk.
For dessert, organic Swedish Fish.
No one here could afford this.
We clear our table, hug
before she leaves. Affirmed
and recharged, we return
to our chores. Me to my register.
She to her home, postpartum.

LAMENT

—to my nephews

You'll never sneak away
to a comic book rack
in the back of a grocery store
—never squeal
at that first squeaky turn
of the prayer wheel.
As a kid, comic books

were a reward for shopping.
I pined for the wet scent
of ink on newsprint,
the glossy, skin-
tight superheroes,
dangerously beautiful
in their poison hues.

Your grandpa read comics
fresh off the farm,
windswept and wild-eyed.
Before you were born,
I hadn't processed the loss
to the imagination—
first generation in five

who wouldn't recognize
these revolving
columns of Valhalla,
their colorful crucibles.
To think, I've spent years
spinning these racks
of masks one last time.

Mid-Shift

The parking lot flushes blood-
orange in the evening sun.
This white guy moseys through

my line, clean-shaven, quiet,
gestures to my pussy hat and asks,
Zachary, what's your solution

to all these terrorist attacks?
Which ones? I ask. All of them,
he says, watching me double-

bag his Hot Bar boxes. Well, I say,
we need to detox masculinity.
What do you mean? he stammers,

Everywhere? Are you Mormon?
Thanks, I say, bagging his receipt.
You're not looking for real

answers, he tells me, backing away.
Toxic masculinity? he cries out,
laughing across the parking lot.

ROSE-MARIE'S MAN-HANDS

Rose-Marie's been asked out
by customers every shift
since she started. Very sexy men
have given her their numbers.
She's nice, but she doesn't like it.
Everyone who works here
crushes on her too, including me.

Too bad she has a boyfriend.
I love her strawberry-blonde mop,
that doe-eyed smolder thing she does,
her vaguely pagan earrings.
Do I want her or want to be her?
My unwary competitor
for male attention. I've read her

palms but couldn't tell much
from all the stress lines.
Her Venus Mound looks like a bird
scratched it to hell. Her fingers
are slender, un-manicured.
She plays James Taylor on guitar.
I do not hate her. I do not hate her.

How to Take an Hour Break

Volunteer to take lunch last.
If no one's waiting on you
to take their break,
no one's tracking your time.
Log in and out,
but stay on the clock.
If someone suspects you,
blame the computer.
Then, unceremoniously
take your break. Eat lunch
outside if you can.
Out of sight, out of mind.
20 minutes later, log in
to 'track your break.'
Now, clock out.
Take half-an-hour
to walk around the block.
Lie out in the afternoon sun.
When Luke's around
picking up his paycheck,
we hotbox his car.
Payroll deducts a lunch
whether or not you take it.
30 minutes later, clock back in,
nod to the boss, then take 10
on company time to shit.

WALKING WHILE WHITE

When Ronnie and I clock-
out at the same time,
we walk the five blocks
to the employee parking lot
together in the dark,
bitching about managers
or riffing off our star-charts.

Everything but the bars is
shut down around us
like a movie set, glowing
coldly under a summer moon.
We cut down the alley,
past the backdoors
of bistros and boutiques,

exiting into streetlight
at a five-way intersection.
We laugh about white folks
thinking her hair is real,
or straight guys flirting gay.
Across from the lot,
I look both ways, decide

there's time, and cross.
Oh, she says, I didn't know
we were walking while white.
We part at her car,
still laughing abstractly,
then like the washed-out stars,
drive away from each other.

4.
Loose Ends

RED DOOR

He buried the placenta
somewhere out in the garden,
Jocelyne said. He was afraid
of what I might do with it.
After two decades, she loved
the house more than her marriage.
Maybe she always had.

They met in '64, hairdressers
in Birmingham, Jocelyne
fresh off a plane from France.
In the 70s, they moved to Nashville,
styling hair and make-up
for a burgeoning film industry
that dried up by the Reagan years.

They restored a late-Victorian
west of the railroad tracks,
abandoned for decades.
Kids had broken in, broke windows.
Squatters had cooked through
the kitchen floor. A door
propped-up the front porch.

After the divorce,
Jocelyne started her own salon
in the basement, feeding
the hair to her plants.
Her mangroves are twice my age.
Color is one of her powers.
Look for the red door.

THE ATTIC

Some faerie from New York
first showed me Jocelyne's attic

years before I lived here,
promptly offering to suck my dick.

Otherwise, I wouldn't dare
go upstairs, certainly not the attic.

But as a resident, I do
occasionally get into antics

in the attic, if it's vacant.
Mostly, browsing the ecstatic

hats handstitched from men's ties!
J's been renovating the attic

for years, her secret apartment.
Open-air shower, thematic

stained-glass window of a bare ass.
Lights thread the plastic

tarp that seals in the ceiling.
I pined for an attic

as a military brat, but couldn't
have conjured this magic.

Faerie Potluck

Once a month, we convene
to eat each other's food,
to gossip, network, and flirt.
We trade in names like Indigo,
Bam-Bam, Constellation.
We wear gay apparel
and last night's eyeshadow.

We come to commune
with unity, to stand in a circle
unbroken for a moment.
Thumbs to the left. Breathe.
Know this, the myths are true:
faerie circles alter you.
Returned to the world, you pay

a different kind of attention.
You may not move into
a commune, but you'll know
conformity as commodity.
See, you've always been fae,
like glitter in the mirror
on your face all day.

Vanishing Act

Jocelyne really wanted us
to go to her neighbor's party,
reappearing in a lavender
trench and pink beret,
cradling assorted leftovers.
She crossed dark yards,
saying in her French accent,
This is the best way.
We kept up, clinging
sheepishly to each other.

The party was lively,
cosmopolitan: dancing
and Latin jazz in the parlor,
booze in the kitchen.
We lost Jocelyne immediately.
Wine in hand, we perused
the cheese; her fuchsia boots
swinging into view
to cheers from the men.
Walking closer, we saw her

slip out the screen door,
sit on the porch,
then drift out into the grass,
past the solitary tree.
Jocelyne? I sang quietly,
but she was already
invisible, a cat, the wind.
We sprinted into the yard
like Mulder and Scully,
but she was gone.

LUKE LEAVES FOR NEW YORK

I knew we shouldn't live
and work together.
We waited till he moved
to the other store.
I generally don't befriend
straight men, unless
I'm trying to sleep with them.

Luke at least has good
taste in music, art,
a good sense of humor,
and he brings his own weed.
Now, he's leaving
for New York, a year queerer,
a weirdo among faeries,

dancing, marching,
doodling cubist spaceships.
(The ayahuasca was his.)
And although no one cares,
here's to you, Luke,
finally swimming nude
with the rest of us.

FALSE BUDDHA

My body glows with the numb calm
of detachment. I've let it all go.
Rage. Envy. Especially of anyone
who can afford to shop here. I don't want
their lives, churning with unresolved
trauma, coffee, and quinoa
(ethically sourced when it's on sale),

their righteous, American guilt,
flash-fried, freeze-dried. I wipe cold sweat
from gluten-free, cashew-cheese
frozen pizzas. I ask easy questions.
Did you find everything okay, today?
Did you know bulk is 10% off on Tuesdays?
The answers don't matter.

I do my best to banter. Bad jazz
blasts overhead. I double-bag 12-packs
of water. This is all so absurd.
I've chosen to stay, though no one
can see me floating here
cross-legged behind this register,
my gold robes licking the air like fire.

Professor Plum

Cleaning, cracking jokes
with another cashier,
I turned to find a former
student standing in line
like Christmas Past.
It was slow, close to closing.
I was halfway into

my bit—How're you?
Find everything okay, today?—
before I recognized him.
Oh, how *are* you? I laughed,
reaching for his groceries.
Eyebrows frowning,
he smiled, landed

his basket with a shrug.
How're *you?* he asked.
Oh, you know, working
to feed my teaching habit.
I opened one paper bag
inside another, *thwap!*
He studied me carefully

bagging his groceries,
his professor. Last semester,
he came-out to me
in his final essay.
I wish I could answer
his face, wish I had more
than bags to hand him.

MERMAIDS

Amiin and I are mermaids.
We've been underwater
so long, we've grown gills.
This deep, you're dead
or you suffer the pressure.
We get a lot of both in here.
The drowned don't know

they're dead. Mermaids
have to navigate the bodies.
We've learned to play-
dead when we meet them.
By that, I mean, we grin
whether we want to or not.
Amiin used to cashier

but moved to the Juice Bar,
where we talk about men
with our eyes. He makes me
smoothies I don't pay for.
I don't charge him for meals.
Your instinct is to thrash
or cry out, but you breathe.

STILL-LIFE

Storm clouds pound the parking lot all
afternoon. On the frontend windows,
10-foot-tall post-it-note tulips cast 8-
bit shadows. Mid-shift left pink kitten
stickers all over my register. The new
kid hands me his latest, self-produced
LP—shirtless on the cover, fake tribal
tattoo on his chest. I turn the radio to
Prince. Finally, they let me leave early.
My apron loosens its noose. We used
to take our nametags home. Now, we
clip them together in the junk-drawer.
When we're not at work keeping them
apart, they lie face-to-face all night.

HIRING FOR MANAGER

Kree came in for groceries
on her day off, and Ms. Sadie
shamed her in front of customers
for wearing a sundress.
Kree came to work
in a red jumpsuit and boots,
and Barb from HR said she'd never
seen her look so *masculine*.
Once, after closing,
Kree asked me to wait for her

to change in the bathroom.
She was meeting friends
at a honkytonk. Sure, I said.
I don't remember
and it doesn't matter
what Kree was wearing
when she came out,
but Carl went on and on
about how good she looked.
He wouldn't stop. It was gross.

And sad. He's married.
I walked her to her truck.
Stars sharpened in the haze.
I asked if she was okay,
but she was months away
from telling me all the sick shit
Carl said to her at work,
before he promoted Luke instead.
Well, she said, wish me luck!
Be safe, I said and waved.

COUNTING MY TILL

After every shift, cashiers
carry our tills upstairs
and count out the cash
on adding machines.
A manager has to sign-off
on the receipt before
you can leave. If you're
more than a few bucks off,
more than a few times,
you're fired. I'm never off.
Third best in the store,
since they fired Kree
and promoted her stalker.
We all quit after that.

This is my last till.
The office watches over
workers on the floor
like the Eye of Mordor.
Normally, it's dead up here.
Today, there's a meeting.
Someone's been watching
porn on this computer,
one manager announces.
The all-female team
(since Carl got Director)
crowds around the screen.
They fired Kree for him.
But who could it be?

Masc

I'm scared and tired
of you, America.
I hide because I can
in plain view.
I grow my own beard.
I wear jeans
I don't want to.
See me grip the seams
like a dress, walking
away from you.

NOTES

Numerology informs the entire collection, particularly multiples of 7. Within each poem, stanzas divide evenly (with one exception).

Many of the poems are sonnets (14 lines), "sonnets.5" (21 lines), and double sonnets (28 lines).

"The Circle-Jerk Boys" riffs on a traditional 4/4 ballad: four stresses to a line, four lines to a stanza.

"The French House" is for Jocelyne Bezzi.

"French House: Sapphics" is modeled after Sappho.

"The Attic" isn't even my best, bad ghazal.

"Vanishing Act" is for Jessie Angel.

For those whose names I didn't change.

ACKNOWLEDGMENTS

My sincerest thanks to the journals and magazines that first published some of these poems:

Echolocation — "Mermaids"
Harpur Palate — "Professor Plum"
Peace, Land, & Bread — "Buffalo Nickel"
Plenitude — "A Body in the Dark"
Qwerty — "Sisters (2)"
RFD — "Kree"
"The Circle-Jerk Boys"
"Johnny from Deli"
"Luke Leaves for New York"
"Masc"
Sixfold — "Facing"
"False Buddha"
"Bagging"
"After the Lunch Rush"
"Liberty Head Nickel"
Zone 3 — "Head Cashier"
"Customer Service"
"My Pink Pussy Hat"

I'm grateful for the love and support of my mother, sister, and many others. In memory of Anna Kirwan.

Activist, educator, musician, and prize-winning poet, Sugar le Fae (PhD) has taught English and writing for two decades; served as a Poetry Editor for *Five Points* (2020), *PRISM international* (2013), and other literary journals; and published widely across North America.

Follow Sugar on Instagram @sugar_lefae.

www.ingramcontent.com/pod-product-compliance
Lightning Source LLC
Chambersburg PA
CBHW011225120626
46545CB00010B/3157